EATING DISORDERS

EATING DISORDERS

Ruth Bjorklund

Marshall Cavendish
Benchmark
New York

With thanks to Rose Calderon, Ph.D., Associate Professor at the University of Washington's Division of Child and Adolescent Psychiatry, and Clinical Director of the Eating Disorders Program at the Children's Hospital and Regional Medical Center in Seattle, for her expert review of the manuscript.

Marshall Cavendish Benchmark
99 White Plains Road
Tarrytown, New York 10591-9001
www.marshallcavendish.us

Library of Congress Cataloging-in-Publication Data

Bjorklund, Ruth.
  Eating disorders / by Ruth Bjorklund.— 1st ed.
      p. cm. — (Health alert)
  Summary: "Discusses eating disorders and their effects on people and
society"—Provided by publisher.
  Includes index.
  ISBN 0-7614-1914-4
  1. Eating disorders—Juvenile literature. I. Title. II. Series: Health alert (Benchmark Books)

  RC552.E18B52 2005
  616.85'26—dc22   2005005782

Photo research by Candlepants, Inc.
Front cover: Ian Boddy/Science Photo Library/Photo Researchers Inc.
The photographs in this book are used by permission and through the courtesy of: *Photoresearchers, Inc.:* Maximilian Stock Ltd., 3, 11; Scott Camazine, 18; Sophie Jacopin, 20; Science Photo Library / Gusto, 22; Science Photo Library, 30; Science Photo Library / Oscar Burriel, 33; Science Photo Library / Jim Varney, 43; Sheila Terry, 45; Carolyn A. McKeone, 49; Science Photo Library / Mauro Fermariello, 50; Science Photo Library / Ed Young, 52. *Picturequest:* Photodisc / Ryan McVay, 16; Photodisc, 19. *Corbis:* Alinari Archives, 27; Chris Hellier, 28; SABA / Shepard Sherbell, 29; Bettmann, 36. *Getty Images:* Tim Graham, 40. *Superstock:* PhotoAlto, 53. *USDA Center for Nutrition Policy and Promotion:* 13.

Printed in China
6 5 4 3 2 1

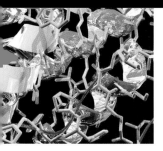

CONTENTS

WHAT IS IT LIKE TO HAVE AN EATING DISORDER?

Julie remembers the terrible day that it all began. She was just eight and on a camping trip in California, while her brothers fished in a mountain stream and her parents stoked the campfire, a stranger grabbed Julie and tried to pull her into the bushes. In one way, she was lucky—her screams allowed her brothers to find her and pull the man away from her. Julie was able to run to safety and her parents, but her world was never the same again.

"I had always been the family princess," explains Julie. "My parents adored me—I was perfect, they thought I could do no wrong." But after Julie's dreadful experience, family life changed. "None of us really talked about the attack," Julie says sadly, "but I felt I wasn't anybody's princess anymore and I no longer believed I was perfect." What Julie did feel was frightened, lonely, abused, and insignificant. People with constant feelings such as these are said to suffer from **depression** and low **self-esteem.** She felt unwanted and withdrew from her family and avoided her friends at school. Julie tried to comfort herself and fill her sadness with food.

"I gained sixty pounds in six months. My mother took me to a weight-loss class when I was just ten years old." No one realized that Julie had developed a serious condition called an eating disorder. An eating disorder is a complicated illness that develops when a person tries to cope with problems in life by starving or overeating. While Julie suffered in silence, she ate. "Nobody figured out that all that weight I put on was because of the 'weight' of my trauma." (A trauma is a deep emotional shock, such as the attack, that has a lasting effect on a person.)

Julie continued to eat. She hid food under her bed, in the back of her closets, and under the clothes in her dresser drawers. When she ate, she ate in secret. Julie **binged,** which meant that she ate huge amounts of food. "I could sit in my room and eat ten candy bars in a row and then go out and buy a half gallon of ice cream and eat that." Julie was out of control. Finally, she decided to lose weight, but she could not bear to give up her secret stashes of food. So she continued to binge. But afterward, she would lock herself in the bathroom and force herself to vomit, to rid herself of the food she ate. This is called **purging.** Julie's eating disorder developed into an even more serious eating disorder called **bulimia nervosa.**

It was a painful way to live. Her body ached from bingeing and vomiting. But because Julie lost weight, people noticed and gave her compliments. The more they noticed, the more Julie wanted to please them. She mistakenly thought that the way to "fit in" better with people was to be thinner. She felt like she was in control of her life and her body. Julie now shakes her head, "Back then, I could walk out of a bathroom teary-eyed and red faced from vomiting and people would tell me I looked pretty. I couldn't believe it!" All the flattery and attention encouraged Julie to continue with her harmful and disordered eating habits.

Throughout her teen years and into her adulthood, Julie binged and purged. And she managed to do this all in secret, without anybody noticing. Sometimes, she would stop bingeing, and instead would starve herself completely. For two years, Julie avoided eating dinner with her family, and turned down invitations from friends that involved food. Some days she allowed herself to eat just one scrambled egg per day. But sometimes she believed that the egg was too much food, and she would purge. Julie lost even more weight and became even thinner. After a year of eating poorly, Julie became dangerously underweight. "I was so thin then," Julie recalls, "but I still thought I weighed too much. I wasn't perfect yet."

Julie was a good student. She earned a college degree, married, and had children. It was not until her second child was born that Julie really tried to get medical help for her eating disorder. A team of doctors, **therapists,** counselors, family, and friends helped Julie resist the urge to control her weight by starving or purging. She learned to eat openly with others and not in secret, and she learned to eat a healthy and reasonable amount of food. She stopped purging. To this day, Julie is not completely rid of her eating disorder. Whenever she feels challenged, sad, anxious, or out of place, she still thinks longingly about bingeing and purging. But Julie manages to control the urge to binge and purge. She finds ways to express her anxious or unhappy feelings in a healthy manner—not by changing her eating habits.

Looking back, Julie can see that her childhood trauma changed her life. She no longer felt good about herself and she felt that others did not care about her either. Quietly, on her own, she tried to heal the emptiness inside by eating. She tried to make herself more attractive to others by losing weight and becoming thin. After many painful years, Julie was fortunately able to leave most of her eating disorders behind, but not without help from a loving family, concerned friends, and thoughtful caregivers.

There are many different types of eating disorders and people can develop these disorders for a variety of reasons. As in Julie's case, a serious trauma may cause an eating disorder. But eating disorders can also be caused by other factors. For example, many young people and teenagers sometimes feel awkward or out of place among their friends and classmates. They may want to be noticed or to be more popular, but cannot figure out how to belong. So they try to make themselves more appealing by losing weight. Some eating disorders develop because of a person's feelings of powerlessness. A person may try to take control of his or her life by managing weight through starvation, bingeing, or purging. Other people suffer from eating disorders as a result of athletic pressure, such as trying to stay in shape for competitive sports.

Regardless of the type and how a person develops it, an eating disorder is a very serious problem. Disordered eating habits can cause severe emotional and physical problems—and some can even lead to death. But knowledge, support, and the proper medical treatment can help many people deal with these disorders.

2

WHAT IS AN EATING DISORDER?

"It's not about the food, it is about control."
—therapist Jeni Gregory

An eating disorder is a complex illness. Most medical experts say that although food and body image are the most noticeable features of an eating disorder, the illness is really about a person's deep **psychological,** social, or emotional conflicts as well as a person's **genetic** makeup. Who will get the disease is not clearly predictable, but many of those that suffer from an eating disorder share common traits. There is also a tendency for an eating disorder to run in families.

Nearly seven million girls and young women in the United States have an eating disorder. In addition, another 15 percent of the population has seriously unhealthy attitudes and habits relating to food. Medical professionals sadly report that there are many more people with eating disorders left uncounted, because so many hide their disease and never seek health care.

A growing number of American boys and men—approximately one million—also develop eating disorders. Nearly all cases occur in the United States, Canada, and parts of Europe and Asia.

EATING WELL

To understand the effects of an eating disorder, it is important to know how to eat normally and well. When people eat normally, they eat at regular times, such as three meals a day, with one to two snack times. They control, or manage, what they eat by eating when hungry and stopping when full. At holiday meals or other fun, social events, healthy eaters sometimes eat more, but it does not become a habit. Eating well means eating food for health and energy. **Nutritious** food also helps people to

The human body needs nutrients in order to function properly. We provide our bodies with these nutrients through the food and beverages that we take in.

think clearly, to keep their moods in balance, and to help them have positive relationships with family and friends.

Food is made of chemical compounds called nutrients. The body needs the nutrients to grow, to fight disease, and to make energy. Basic nutrients are proteins, carbohydrates, fats, vitamins, and minerals. Carbohydrates are the body's fuel source. Fats keep the skin from drying out, protect organs, and insulate the body against the cold. Proteins build and mend muscle. Various vitamins and minerals are also part of a balanced diet. They help keep the body healthy and its systems in good repair.

Food groups contain different amounts of nutrients. The five food groups are grains, fruits, vegetables, dairy, and meat (including poultry, fish, beans, eggs, and nuts). To be healthy, a person needs proper servings from each group each day. When people eat, their bodies convert food into energy. A scientific unit called a kilocalorie measures this energy. In everyday conversation, kilocalorie is shortened to **calorie.** American schoolchildren ages seven to ten should consume about 2,000 calories a day. A teenage girl should consume about 2,000 calories per day and a teenage boy, about 2,500 to 3,000 calories. If a teen is involved in very vigorous activities, extra calories are necessary. It should be noted, however, that these are average numbers. Your family doctor or a nutritionist can help you determine what is the right amount and type of food for you.

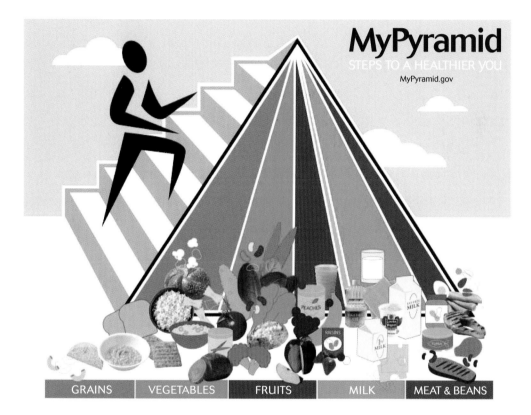

In 2005, the United States Department of Agriculture (USDA) unveiled a brand-new food pyramid. The new pyramid is a guide to wholesome eating. To eat a balanced diet, most people need about 1,500 to 2,500 calories a day, depending on how active they are. Meals should include healthy servings of whole grains, fruits, vegetables, dairy products, and protein foods such as meat, nuts, eggs, and beans. If you are curious about balanced diets, your family doctor, a school nurse, or a nutritionist can help you figure out how many calories you need each day.

There are several types of eating disorders. The three most common are **anorexia nervosa,** bulimia nervosa, and binge-eating disorder. All of these diseases show signs of an abnormal and unhealthy relationship with food and eating, and sometimes with physical exercise.

Anorexia Nervosa

The Greek word *anorexia* and the Latin word *nervosa* together mean "loss of appetite for nervous reasons." Anorexia nervosa is often simply called anorexia. People who suffer from anorexia actually ignore their appetite, rather than lose it. They are hungry all the time, but they severely limit what they eat and drink. People with anorexia are terrified of gaining weight and eat so little food that their bodies become malnourished and frail.

Studies show that 99 percent of teens with anorexia are girls. People who become anorexic can be of any age, size, race, culture, religion, or ethnic group. Most are outwardly model students, well behaved, perfection seeking, and eager to please. But inside, as the illness grows, these young people become insecure, anxious, lonely, and depressed. Most who develop anorexia do so at **puberty,** when their adolescent bodies begin maturing into adulthood. Weight gain is a healthy and necessary part of this process. An average girl living in the United States between the ages of 8 and 14 can normally expect to gain about 40 pounds in that time. Yet for those who develop anorexia, the extra pounds are reason for alarm.

The disease often starts during a period of difficult change. Usually, it occurs in adolescence (ages 10 to 18), but it can happen at any age. Sometimes, a deeply disturbing episode triggers the onset of the disease, such as an attack. Sometimes, school and personal commitments become overwhelming. Dr. Rosemary Calderon, a Seattle **psychologist** explains, "Some of the teenagers simply have too many balls in the air. They get straight A's, they're the prom queen, the soccer captain, they do charity work, and they have a relationship with a boyfriend. It's too much. They can't function at that high a level all the time." Other demands, such as another family member's health problems, divorce, alcoholism, drug abuse, broken friendships, or even a misguided insult can send a person into emotional turmoil. Suddenly, the world spins painfully out of control.

People with anorexia try to handle the chaos they feel inside by taking complete control of the size and shape of their bodies. They develop strict rules for themselves about how much food they will eat, where, when, and with whom. People with anorexia **obsessively** count calories, weigh themselves several times a day, and skip eating meals. When others notice their weight loss and praise them for it, people with anorexia are encouraged to continue their anorexic behaviors. They become

One way people monitor their caloric intake (the number of calories they eat or drink) is by reading food labels. People with anorexia, however, often become obsessed with counting the calories they take in.

proud of their self-control. Often, they feel superior to their friends that eat normally. As a person who once struggled with the disease says, "I didn't want to be better than anyone; I wanted to be better than *everyone!*"

People with anorexia have troubles that they cannot control, so in order to control something, they control their weight. However, before long, their weight control becomes their most distressing problem. Most people with anorexia are at least 15 percent below a normal body weight for their body type. Yet they continue to believe they are "too fat." As their illness progresses, many use other self-destructive tactics in their battle against unwanted pounds. Some overexercise. They may run miles and miles everyday, despite bad weather or how weak their bodies feel. Others frantically do sit-ups in the middle of the night to try and "work off" what few calories they consumed during the day. After eating and feeling guilty for doing so, some force themselves to vomit. Others abuse drugs such as **diuretics, laxatives,** and diet pills. A diuretic drug rids the body of water by causing frequent urination. Laxatives increase **bowel** movements to rid the body of fecal waste. Diet pills speed up the body's metabolism and reduce feelings of hunger. People with the most serious cases of anorexia often use a combination of these behaviors.

People with anorexia do not get enough nutrients to keep their bodies healthy. Their bodies begin to collapse. First, by lacking proper nutrition, they become tired and weak. They may faint or have frequent headaches. Their digestive systems slow and they suffer stomach and intestinal pains. Because they eat little or no fat, the protective layers of fat under their skin and around their organs disappear, causing them to shiver from cold, even in warm weather. Because they are constantly cold, fine hairs called *lanugo* sprout all over their bodies in an effort to provide warmth. Their skin dries and their hair falls out. Young women with anorexia often experience problems with their reproductive system.

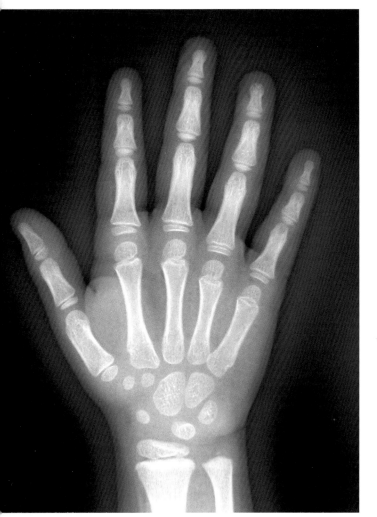

As adults, humans have more than 200 bones in the body. Bones are designed to support the body and allow it to move. However, eating disorders can make bones brittle and frail—and very easy to break.

Most sufferers tend to ease their appetite by drinking large amounts of diet soda, which prevents their bodies from absorbing calcium. Without calcium, bones become brittle. Because they eat so few calories, people with anorexia have nothing to convert into energy. To produce energy, their bodies burn muscle tissue. In time, they can appear to be virtually skin and bone. Their heart rate drops, their liver and kidneys fail. People who go untreated for this disease are at risk of serious permanent injury, or death.

Bulimia Nervosa

The phrase, *bulimia nervosa,* is from two Greek words together meaning the "appetite of an ox" and the Latin word *nervosa,* meaning "for nervous reasons." Bulimia nervosa, then, is a disease of overeating combined with emotional, social, physical, or mental stress. The disease is similar to anorexia nervosa in that the disordered eating usually begins around puberty, is suffered more by females than males, and is commonly triggered by family or social problems.

People who suffer from bulimia binge and eat huge amounts of food during a short period. Then they purge

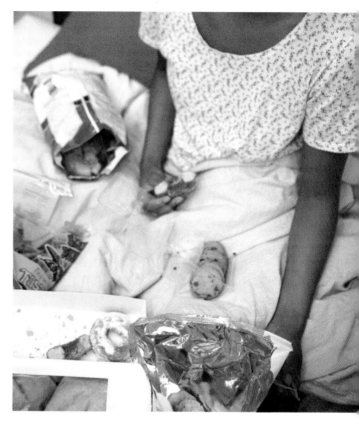

Binge eaters often hoard and eat their food in secret.

to rid their bodies of the food. Bulimia is sometimes called binge-purge syndrome. Some people with bulimia eat twenty to twenty-five times the recommended daily calories for their body type. Most people with bulimia end their bouts of over-eating by forcing themselves to vomit. Others use drugs such as laxatives, diuretics, and diet pills. Some anxiously exercise to burn the calories they have consumed. Still others attempt anorexic-like **fasts.**

But there are distinct differences between the two disorders. People with bulimia are not noticeably thin. Many, in fact, are slightly overweight. Their binge-purge strategies fall short at successful weight loss because they often consume more in their binges than it is possible to purge. People with bulimia are extremely secretive. They stockpile food and keep it out of sight. They also hide the evidence of their binges, such as cleaning up dirty dishes or burying empty cereal boxes under other household trash. They make quick exits from the table to use the bathroom to purge. Unlike people with anorexia, who often feel proud of their strict fasting, persons with bulimia are generally very ashamed of their behavior. "It is a disease of great secrecy," says therapist Jeni Gregory.

People with bulimia do enormous injury to their bodies. They regularly suffer from stomach and intestinal pains. In addition, because of their vomiting, they often have swollen glands in the face and neck, headaches, and burst blood vessels in the eyes. Their constant bingeing and purging weakens the heart. Harsh stomach acids also do serious damage. When they vomit their food, the acids wash up the esophagus (the muscular tube that connects the throat to the stomach), and into the mouth. This causes a burning feeling in the esophagus; a raw, sore throat; painful, bleeding gums; and the erosion of tooth enamel, which leads to rotting teeth.

The use of laxatives and diuretics also leads to multiple health problems. People with bulimia and anorexia who use these drugs lose too much body fluid and become **dehydrated.** This can lead to seizures in the brain. (Seizures are disturbances in the brain that cause uncontrollable movements and loss of consciousness.) Their skin turns flaky and dry. Bowels, liver, and kidneys often suffer permanent damage. Unchecked and untreated, sufferers do themselves irreversible harm and may die from complications of their disorder. Health-care providers warn that a person who suffers from both anorexia and bulimia has an extremely grim, life-threatening condition.

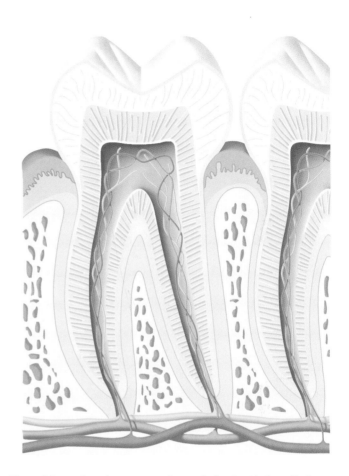

The white-colored, outer surface of the teeth is called enamel. It is a strong substance that protects the teeth and allows you to chew different types of food. But stomach acid from frequent vomiting can wear down and destroy the enamel. This can lead to tooth decay.

Binge-eating Disorder

Binge-eating disorder is also called **compulsive overeating** disorder. Binge-eating disorder is somewhat like bulimia, except

that those who suffer from the disease do not try to purge their food. Many people who have binge-eating disorders rapidly consume excessive amounts of food during a short period, often in secret. Others eat almost constantly, with large amounts at mealtimes, and snacks throughout the day. They do not eat because of hunger, but as a way of trying to cope with daily problems. Most binge-eaters are overweight. Many are **obese.** Being a few pounds overweight is not the same as being obese. An obese person is very overweight and has a very large amount of extra body fat.

Frequently eating large amounts of foods that are high in fats can harm the body. An unhealthy diet may cause obesity, heart problems, and diseases like diabetes.

Binge-eaters do harm to their bodies by their irregular and extreme eating habits. Though they often try diets, they do not follow them as strictly as people with anorexia or bulimia do. Their up-and-down weight changes and their large and unbalanced meals cause shifts in their **metabolism,** making it difficult for their bodies to convert food into energy. Binge-eaters also develop other serious medical problems. When they gain too much weight, they put an unhealthy stress on the heart and circulatory system (which circulates nutrient-rich blood through-out the body). They may also develop high blood pressure, high cholesterol, or diabetes, which is a disease of the pancreas. People who binge-eat just their favorite foods, such as ice cream or potato chips, risk becoming dangerously malnourished. Of all the eating disorders, binge-eating disorder is the most common. Nearly 5 percent of Americans suffer from the disease.

Other Eating Disorders

There are a few other eating disorders. One is called, *anorexia athletica,* which is also known as "compulsive exercising disorder." A person with this disorder repeatedly overexercises in order to lose weight. There are some other rare eating disorders. Among them are night eating disorder, Prader-Willi Syndrome, and pica. In night-eating disorder, a person binges while sleepwalking. The binge-eating disorder known as Prader-Willi Syndrome is caused by a genetic flaw. (Prader-Willi Syndrome also has a number of other distinctive features that are unrelated to binge-eating.) With pica, affected people have an uncontrol-lable urge to consume non-foods such as chalk, clay, coins, or soap. *Pica* is a Latin word for magpie, a bird that likes to eat shiny bits of metal and other objects it finds.

Signs and Symptoms of Eating Disorders

Many different eating disorders share similar symptoms, though they are separate disorders. This chart can help you identify the main symptoms of three major eating disorders.

ANOREXIA NERVOSA

- Extreme weight loss
- Sensitive to cold
- Growth of *lanugo*
- Dry skin, brittle nails
- Amenorrhea (absence of menstrual periods)
- Low self-esteem
- Fainting
- Abuse of laxatives, diuretics, or diet pills
- Damage to teeth and gums
- Disappearing regularly into the bathroom after eating
- Withdrawal from family, friends, and activities
- Unusual eating habits—taking small bites, skipping meals, eating in secret, throwing uneaten food away
- Negative body image—think of themselves as "fat" when in fact they are very thin. Wears baggy clothes to hide body
- Weighs oneself frequently
- Overexercises

BULIMIA NERVOSA

- Up and down changes in weight
- Damage to teeth and gums
- Swollen glands, sore throat
- Bloodshot eyes
- Low self-esteem
- Mood swings
- Abuse of laxatives, diuretics, or diet pills
- Disappearing regularly into the bathroom after eating
- Withdrawal from family, friends, and activities
- Eats large amounts of food in short period of time
- Eats in secret, hoards and stashes food
- Negative body image
- Weighs oneself frequently

BINGE-EATING DISORDER

- Weight gain
- Quickened heart rate
- Eats rapidly
- Eats alone
- Low-self-esteem
- Depression
- Dizziness
- Withdrawal from family, friends, and activities
- Eats large amounts of food in short period of time
- Hoards and stashes food
- Negative body image

3

EATING DISORDERS THROUGH TIME

Although eating disorders did not seem to be in the public eye until the middle of the twentieth century, forms of the disease have plagued humans through the ages. Around 480 BCE, a Greek historian named Herodotos traveled throughout the Mediterranean. In ancient Egypt, he came across people practicing a ritualistic form of bulimia. He wrote of the Egyptians, "for three successive days in each month they purge the body by means of **emetics** . . . for they think that it is from the food they eat that all sicknesses come to men." (An emetic is a solution that when taken, will cause vomiting.)

In ancient Rome, the Emperors dispatched their armies around the world. Roman soldiers discovered foods of other lands and brought them home. Roman nobles enjoyed feasting to excess on these new delights. Many would eat until full, and then purge to empty the stomach so that the feasting could continue. Some historians believe that it was customary for Romans to build a room called a "vomitorium" near banquet halls. These side-by-side facilities allowed the nobles to binge in the banquet hall, use the vomitorium to purge, and then continue eating. (Other sources claim that a vomitorium was actually a passageway and not a room for vomiting. So it is possible that early Romans used a vomitorium to move from room to room to binge and purge.)

In the Middle Ages (500 CE to 1500 CE), a disease physicians called *anorexia miribilus* became known. The term means "loss of appetite for miraculous reasons." Mainly, devoutly religious persons suffered from this condition. They fasted in order to achieve spiritual perfection.

An Italian painting (by Bernardino Fungai) of Catherine of Siena.

Some became saints, including Catherine of Siena, a nun who lived on just a few herbs a day. She ultimately died of starvation.

In 1689, an English physician named Richard Morton wrote about a patient who had what he termed "a wasting disease of nervous origins." The young woman had "a multitude of cares and passions of the mind" and refused to eat. She was but "a

Besides being the first to use the term *anorexia nervosa*, Sir William Gull also identified diseases that affect other organs, such as the thyroid and kidneys.

skeleton clad only with skin." In 1873, a French doctor named Charles Lasegue wrote about a patient of his who refused to eat and was overcome with "hysteria." The following year, another English doctor, Sir William Gull, reported having a patient with similar symptoms. He coined the medical term *anorexia nervosa*.

In 1979, a British doctor named Gerald Russell wrote a paper describing bulimia nervosa as a separate disease from anorexia nervosa. He wrote, ". . . the patient suffers from powerful urges to overeat; the patient seeks to avoid the 'fattening' effects of food by inducing vomiting or abusing purgatives or both; the patient has a morbid fear of becoming obese."

In the twentieth century, cases of eating disorders began appearing more frequently. Doctors and researchers looked for a cause. Many first treated the disease as a biological illness— they thought that there was something physically wrong with the body causing the disease. Then in the 1930s, doctors began to regard the disease as having social and psychological causes.

In 1983, anorexia nervosa and other eating disorders gained widespread recognition. A well-known pop singer named Karen Carpenter died from heart failure. She had been secretly anorexic for eight years, so her death was a shock to the public. However, the tragedy helped raise public awareness of the disease, making health care more accessible and new research more possible.

Karen Carpenter's death from heart failure—caused by the strain on her body from her eating disorder—made the public more aware of the dangers of eating disorders.

Biological Causes

In recent years, new scientific studies have shown strong links between eating disorders and genetics. Genetics is the study of how characteristics are passed from parent to child through **genes.** Genes are pieces of chemical information contained in the cells of plants and animals. Genes determine heredity characteristics, such as what eye color, body type, or natural ability a person inherits from his or her parents.

Some studies have found that certain genes carry information that makes a person more likely to develop an eating disorder. Other studies show that a person's chance of developing an eating disorder is about 1 in 200, but if a family member has the disease, that chance increases to 1 in 30. Studies in identical twins show that if one develops anorexia, the other has an almost 50 percent chance of also developing the disease. "It is very clear genetics is a major factor," asserts a researcher at the University of Washington.

Other researchers are looking at chemical messengers in the body that function abnormally in many people with eating disorders. Their studies show that when some people starve or binge, chemicals called endorphins change in their brain, and they feel a sense of peace and happiness, instead of anxiety and depression. (The positive feelings from endorphins, however, do not last for a long time. Also, endorphins can be released naturally, during normal, healthy body processes.) In 2004, researchers discovered a **hormone** (a chemical released by certain cells to act on other parts of the body) that seems to regulate a person's appetite. In an article in *Science* magazine, researchers called the new hormone *leptin,* from a Greek word for "thin." They demonstrated that mice with certain levels of leptin were better able to control their weight than other mice. In studying biological causes of eating disorders, researchers hope to develop medications and therapies to ease the suffering and help cure the disease.

Psychological Causes

"Let me tell you the profile of a typical young woman with an eating disorder," says psychologist Dr. Calderon. "She is smart, caring, a perfectionist and a pleaser; someone who always wants to do the right thing." What happens is that something changes in her life, and she no longer "knows where she belongs." This person once knew where her strengths lay. She once was popular, confident, active, and successful. However, a shift occurs and the person may change schools, for instance,

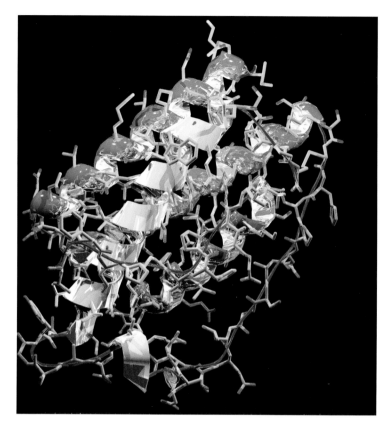

A computer model of leptin. Scientists have found the leptin controls body functions that have to do with bone formation, fat regulation, reproduction, and appetite. Many believe that learning how leptin regulates appetite can help with research dealing with understanding and treating eating disorders.

may move from elementary school to middle school, or high school to college. Suddenly, this person is no longer sure of herself, but she thinks, "I should know how to do this." And yet she does not. She has always set very high standards for herself, and she cannot achieve those high standards in her latest situation. So she retreats. She becomes obsessed with food and her appearance. Before long, she is perfect at something new. She is perfect at starving herself. Deep inside her mind, she senses that being ill is a graceful way of sidestepping the pressure she feels.

People with eating disorders have nearly impossible expectations of themselves and others. It is hard for them to be flexible. They see things only as good or bad. Therapists call this "black or white thinking." "My sister," says a teacher named Tina Raymond, "has been anorexic and bulimic for years. She is an amazing photographer. Of all us in the family, she is the most talented, successful, and determined. When she walks in the room, she completely takes over—my mother calls her 'The General.' But I can't bear to be around her when she eats." In spite of their many successes, people with an eating disorder cannot accept the shape and size of their bodies. They do whatever they can to manage and control what they see about themselves as imperfect.

A person with an eating disorder often carries a negative body image. A body image is a picture formed in the mind about one's appearance. This mental picture may have no basis in fact. In other words, a person can believe himself or herself to be too fat, too thin, too short, too tall, or in some other way, unattractive, when in fact, they do not have shortcomings at all. People with a negative body image may feel badly about themselves one day, but not the next. Others may be unable to think of anything else but their appearance all of the time. By focusing constant attention on their appearance, people who suffer from an eating disorder can avoid the deeper and more complicated issues in their lives. The person with an eating disorder who insists he or she is "too fat," is really saying, "I feel bad."

People with eating disorders often have distorted body images. This means that they see themselves as very fat—even though they are not—and engage in harmful practices like obsessive dieting, starvation, and purging to regulate their weight.

Social and Family Causes and Concerns

According to numerous scientific studies, low self-esteem is a very common trait among people with eating disorders. Self-esteem begins in childhood. It is a feeling of satisfaction with one's achievements, appearance, and abilities. When family and friends love and respect a child, self-esteem is likely to grow. Think of the pride a student feels when a parent displays a drawing or a spelling test on the refrigerator door. That action contributes to the child's self-esteem. As a child moves into his or her teenage years, he or she still needs encouragement. But the teen years are a difficult time. Teens face so many new challenges and changes. Although they are more independent, they still rely on people such as parents, classmates, coaches, teachers, and friends for support. But parents who make difficult demands on their children, classmates who bully and tease, or friends who compare and criticize each other's appearance can destroy a person's self-esteem—at any age.

There are events in family life that can play a part in an eating disorder. Parents who treat food as a frequent reward for good behavior can give their children the wrong idea about healthy eating. If a young person believes food is a reward, then he or she may overeat to try to duplicate the good feeling a reward brings. A person may decide to starve instead, if he or she feels "not good enough." Sometimes, parents are very worried about the unhealthiness of junk food and restrict what their children eat. This may give their children powerful cravings that send them on secret binges. Other serious family problems can upset a child or teen and trigger disordered eating. A person's self-esteem can be damaged by serious disruptions such as separation or divorce; verbal, physical, or sexual abuse; drug abuse or alcoholism.

Outside of the family, other important social relationships can backfire. Good friendships are key to a person's sense of well being and value. Watching a friend move away, or having a friendship fail can make a person's self-confidence falter. Classmates who tease and ridicule can leave lasting damage on their emotionally sensitive peers. One cutting remark can launch a life-threatening bout of anorexic or bulimic behavior. As a young woman with a severe case of anorexia wrote, "It was just a few innocent comments about my weight and body that stung like a bee." The pop star Karen Carpenter embarked on her fatal journey into anorexia after she read a magazine article that described her as being "chubby."

While most eating disorders seem to come from a desire to be more physically attractive, some eating disorders are prompted by a desire to be fit. Young people involved in athletic activities can become eating disordered while trying to be best at their game. Various competitive athletics have weight guidelines—dance, gymnastics, rowing, wrestling, horseback riding, track, and swimming, to name a few. Determined athletes may put themselves on strict diets and exercise to excess. In the 1980s and 1990s, Christy Henrich was a member of the U.S. Gymnastics team. She weighed only 93 pounds when

Eating disorders are common among athletes who participate in competitive sports in which weight and size are important. Nadia Comaneci was an Olympic medal-winning athlete famous for her gymnastic skills. It was later revealed that she struggled with an eating disorder to maintain her small, athletic frame.

a judge at an international competition warned her she needed to watch her weight. Henrich believed that the judge was telling her she was too fat to be an Olympic level gymnast. So she began a rigid weight loss program that progressed to anorexia and bulimia. About her eating disorder Henrich revealed, "It feels like there is a beast inside of me, a monster." Christy Henrich died from her disease in 1994.

Many athletic boys and young men also develop eating disorders. They desire to be strong and muscular. Some overexercise, others overeat, and still others starve themselves to stay lean, but "bulk up" by abusing synthetic (artificial) hormones called anabolic steroids that increase their muscle size.

Cultural Pressures

Society and culture have always influenced how people relate
to the human body. Europeans in the Middle Ages felt large,
ample bodies were desirable. At the time, being large meant
that a person was a wealthy landowner whose fields were able
to produce great quantities of food. Later, in the seventeenth
century, European women stuffed themselves into painful,
tight-fitting steel corsets, in order to force their bodies into
shapes society decided were pleasing. The trend continued to
America. In the nineteenth century, an increasing number of
Americans moved into cities and towns. They purchased their
food in markets and stores. A large-sized person was no longer
assumed to be well-to-do and well-fed. People started to
idealize a thin human shape.

By the 1960s, very thin and lean movie stars and models
covered the pages of magazines and newspapers. Since that
time, tall, thin celebrities with oval shaped faces have
represented Western society's ideal. (Western society is generally
considered to be the countries in Western Europe and their
former colonies where many Europeans settled, such as the
United States, Canada, Mexico, Argentina, Brazil, Australia,
and New Zealand.) Outside Western societies, many cultures
still consider plumpness attractive and desirable. In such
cultures, eating disorders are far less common. This fact leads
many experts to explore theories about how Western culture

Advertising, Eating Disorders, and You

....

Critics of the media say that the driving cause behind the cultural ideal of thinness is money. Corporations make billions of dollars every year selling fashion, cosmetics, and weight-loss programs to people, especially girls and women who desire to be attractive and popular. Many experts recommend that people be careful and watch out for the good and bad in advertising.

GOOD ADS SHOW

- People with a variety of natural body shapes and sizes
- Heavy and thin people alike with positive characteristics
- People eating balanced meals as part of a healthy lifestyle
- Women as more than objects of beauty

OFFENSIVE ADS SHOW

- Excessively thin models
- Models whose features have been computer-enhanced
- Large people who are being ridiculed for their weight or size
- Large people with negative characteristics
- Glamorized stories and images of people who diet

and the media play a role in causing eating disorders.

"I can't believe how many girls wear a size one or three here in the high school," says Becky Deeter, a school nurse. "Girls faint in the halls. I heard one say, 'You have to do what you have to do.' But, they *don't have to!*" Many social pressures from the media and from peers help convince girls and young women that to be popular and attractive, they must be thin. Even girls as young as seven or eight have admitted to trying to diet in order to be thin. "By fifth or sixth grade, you can really see the trouble starting," says Deeter. "The way most teens start on the road to an eating disorder is by going on a diet."

The media has a huge influence on people, especially young people. Fashion magazines are loaded with images of extremely thin supermodels. Every cover promises a fantastic new weight-loss plan. The average fashion model is 5 foot 11 inches tall and weighs less than 120 pounds. Compare that to the average American woman who stands 5 foot 4 inches tall and weighs 140 pounds. The ideal represented by the supermodel is not at all reality. Television and movies also reinforce this image.

These cultural pressures are desperately difficult to ignore. Experts at the National Eating Disorders Association (NEDA) have a contract they would like young people to sign called, *A Declaration of Independence from a Weight-Obsessed World.* NEDA asks young people to accept their natural body shape and size. The contract also asks people to resist society's pressures to judge themselves and others based on physical appearances. Other organizations have run successful protest campaigns against advertisers that glamorize excessively thin people, or ridicule heavy people.

Just as girls and women have impossible ideals of thinness and beauty, so do boys and men. Tall, strong, muscular men symbolized by star athletes and other celebrities represent Western culture's ideal male form. But few males have the ideal body type that is represented in the media's ads, television shows, movies, and sporting events. Boys and young men who suffer from eating disorders are often obsessed with their physical performance and exercise relentlessly. Those who are unable to excel at sports often suffer low self-esteem.

This photograph, taken in 1993, shows Princess Diana heading toward an eating disorders conference in London. During this conference—and at many other events—the princess spoke about her eating disorder and encouraged awareness and action.

Hope for the Future

In the last few decades, reported cases of anorexia, bulimia, and other eating disorders have increased, but so has the medical knowledge. Twenty-first century medical professionals are seeking a greater understanding of eating disorders. They recognize that the disease likely develops from a combination of causes—genetic, psychological, social, and cultural.

Researchers, therapists, and other health-care providers are presently developing new and more advanced therapies to help sufferers battle their complicated and heartbreaking disorder. "A lot of things are happening right now in therapies," reports Dr. Calderon. "There's a big shift. Still no sure cures, but it feels like we are gaining a sense of what is really going on with these patients and how better to help them."

Famous People with an Eating Disorder

Eating disorders can affect anybody anywhere. Included in the percentage of people suffering from eating disorders are celebrities and other famous individuals. Though they struggled in silence for years, many have come forward to share their experiences and problems with the public. This has helped to call attention to the dangers of eating disorders and has shown people that they do not have to struggle alone—help is available. Some of these people include

Yeardley Smith, actress and voice of cartoon character Lisa Simpson

Tracey Gold, actress

Daniel Johns, singer and songwriter

Princess Victoria, Crown Princess of Sweden

Cathy Rigby, Olympic gymnast

Anne Lamott, author

Christina Ricci, actress

Princess Diana, Princess of Wales

Fiona Apple, singer and songwriter

Gelsey Kirkland, ballerina

Jamie-Lynn Discala, actress

Billy Bob Thornton, actor and director

Nadia Comaneci, Olympic gymnast

4

TREATING AN EATING DISORDER

"I tell you, it feels like a small miracle, to have learned to eat . . . " —writer Anne Lamott

An eating disorder is a complicated and serious condition. Rarely does the disorder go away on its own. Many health experts say that the only way for people with an eating disorder to get well is to choose to do so. Doctors call it the "readiness factor."

Researchers say that eating disorders are one of the least likely psychological illnesses to be treated. Yet people who suffer from eating disorders need professional help in order to get well. Therapist Jeni Gregory says that sufferers must realize that they are not alone. They must learn to reach out to other people, whether friends, family, or professional care givers and ask for help and support. Once a person with an eating disorder admits to someone else that food controls his or her life, that act becomes the first and most important step toward recovery.

TREATMENT TYPES

There are many treatments for eating disorders. Most professionals believe that the best treatment is a combination of therapies. Some of the most common treatments are nutrition therapy, **psychotherapy,** (including group and family therapy), and medication. Specialists who practice these therapies are physicians,

Counseling and talk therapy are often used to help people with different types of problems and concerns.

counselors, social workers, dieticians or nutritionists, nurses, and psychotherapists. Together with friends and family, these specialists form a treatment team. It is essential that everyone work together. Some people with eating disorders are outpatients, meaning that they make visits to care providers for treatment, but live at home. Other patients, whose eating disorders are the most severe, become patients in a hospital or residential care facility.

Nutrition Therapy

Before the mind can heal, health-care providers say the body must heal. People with eating disorders have damaged their bodies to such a degree, that they have disturbed the chemistry of their brain. So patients cannot begin psychotherapy to treat their disordered thinking, until they correct their destructive eating. For many, especially those with bulimia or binge-eating disorders, a nutrition therapist plans healthy menus.

Since most people with bulimia or binge-eating disorders are treated on an out-patient basis, friends and family members are an important part of the treatment process. They should make certain the patient eats the prescribed foods. They also must watch patients carefully and keep them busy after a meal. This distracts patients from their concerns about eating and helps prevent secret purges.

For people with anorexia, nutritionists must re-introduce foods. These patients, who have starved themselves into a critical state, can regain strength by working their way from several very small meals over the course of a day to eventually more normal-size meals and snacks after several days. "I tell my patients," says Dr. Calderon, "You don't have to like eating, it can be mechanical. But it is like a cut that must be cleaned and bandaged. Food is the medicine. It is how you heal. You must eat."

Psychotherapy

Psychotherapy is a term that describes treating emotional and mental problems by talking, persuading, suggesting, and reassuring a patient. In this type of therapy, a therapist, psychologist, or social worker works one-on-one with a patient. The professional leads their conversations in directions that help patients see themselves and their problems more clearly. There are many types of psychotherapy used in treating eating disorders.

Medical research has shown that cognitive-behavioral therapy, known as CBT, is often the most successful. In this type of therapy, psychologists or psychiatrists discuss with patients their thoughts about food. Then, the therapists point out strategies to cope with and change their behavior.

Sometimes, therapists ask patients to keep a food journal. The journal helps patients see for themselves what

Fixing their harmful eating habits is very difficult for people suffering from eating disorders. Many of them have eaten this way for much of their lives and changing their routine is not easy.

they eat each day and how they feel while eating. Patterns appear. Patients might notice that bad grades, family arguments, or other disappointments trigger episodes of starving or bingeing. In CBT, therapists teach patients to avoid those triggers, or to recognize them while they occur and make an extra effort to control their unhealthy eating behaviors. Therapists using CBT also encourage patients to recognize that when they say they "feel fat" they are really having a bad day and are feeling another emotion, such as anger or sadness. CBT helps patients learn how they have substituted disordered eating habits for unwanted feelings.

Other important psychotherapies are family therapy and support group therapy. In family therapy, patients and their families gather with a counselor or therapist and discuss issues that are difficult to bring up in everyday family life. Often, these sessions bring family members closer together, and help the patient feel better about himself or herself. Therapist Gregory says it is important that parents learn the language of therapy. They should learn how to talk to their children about important and difficult matters with honesty and caring. Many patients feel unwanted and alone because of their disease. One patient said, "I always felt people loved me, but wouldn't if they knew the truth."

Support group therapy helps with these feelings. Eating disorder support groups are therapy sessions involving other patients with similar problems. Often guided by a therapist or counselor, people in support groups share their feelings about having an eating disorder and struggling to control it. Because people who have an eating disorder usually keep their disease a secret, being able to talk openly with others about their actions improves their self-esteem and helps them to cope. Other psychotherapies are dance, art, hypnosis, movement or body image therapy. In each of these therapies, patients learn to explore positive feelings about themselves and their abilities and learn to focus less on their negative feelings.

Medication Therapy

A medical doctor or a **psychiatrist** can help a person with an eating disorder through medication therapy. There are no medications particularly intended to relieve the symptoms of eating disorders. However, many medications developed to treat depression, anxiety, and mood disorders can be useful in treating eating disorders. Doctors believe that a combination of psychotherapy and medication therapy is the best way to treat people who suffer from anorexia or bulimia.

WHAT HAPPENS DURING TREATMENT

Once it is clear that a person has an eating disorder, family members should act quickly. Early intervention and treatment are key to a healthy recovery. People with serious eating disorders usually deny they have a problem. They do not, and often cannot, seek treatment on their own. That is why sufferers need the help and support of family and friends. Together, they can assemble a team of health-care professionals. The team may include nurses, social workers, psychiatrists, psychologists, nutritionists, and other therapists.

The first treatment should be a complete medical examination. The physician will check all organs such as heart, liver, kidneys, and brain, as well as body systems, such as skeletal, muscular, hormonal, or digestive. Medical staff will begin treating all critical conditions right away. After the examination, the physician will determine whether a patient requires a hospital stay or can be treated as an outpatient. Patients with families willing and able to follow treatment guidelines faithfully often remain at home. Outpatient care is less expensive. So many health insurance companies are reluctant to fund treatment in a hospital or residence care facility. However, despite the cost, doctors will urge hospital or residence facility care if the patient is gravely ill or if problems at home prevent successful treatment.

The next step is to put the patient on track for healthy eating. People with bulimia or binge-eating disorder begin instruction on healthy nutrition. They learn about proteins, carbohydrates, and other nutrients and their roles in keeping the body healthy and strong.

Nutritionists design menus and food choices and patients and their families select healthy foods and eat at regular times in relaxed surroundings. They work together to prevent episodes of purging. Patients with bulimia who are admitted to a special residence or hospital have a schedule to follow during the day. They eat healthful, regular meals, take classes, exercise, and participate in therapy sessions. Many write about their experience in journals. After meals, patients remain together for social activities, while staff members watch carefully to prevent purging or overexercising.

Patients with anorexia begin a more delicate re-feeding process. In extreme cases, when hospitalized patients will not eat, doctors may feed them using a nasogastric (NG) tube. An

NG tube is a tiny tube that is inserted through the patient's nose and extends down the esophagus to the stomach. Liquids vital to survival are delivered through the tube. Patients who make an effort to cooperate often become extremely anxious when they try to eat. To reduce their anxiety, many take **anti-depressant** medications to help them manage the difficult re-feeding stage.

As patients begin to eat in a healthy manner, they become ready for psychotherapy. Outpatients visit their therapists for individual, family, and sometimes group therapy sessions. Visits are frequent, often daily, in the early stages of treatment. Hospital and residence care patients receive daily psychotherapy as soon as their bodies have shown signs of healing. In therapy, therapists talk to their patients and guide their disordered thoughts about food and body

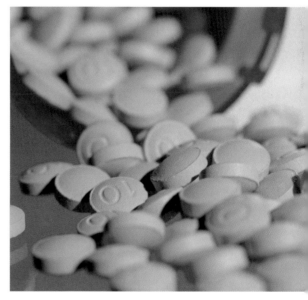

Doctors often prescribe—or order—special anti-depressants to help relieve some of the depression and anxiety that people with eating disorders often feel.

image into more wholesome patterns. They encourage their patients to accept themselves as they are and to make positive and hopeful changes in their lives.

Recovering from an eating disorder is no simple task. It

A counselor helps a young woman suffering from anorexia. She is learning how to eat healthy portions of food on a regular schedule.

takes time and patience. People with eating disorders have numerous other medical complications to bear, such as weakened kidneys, heart, muscles, digestive systems and more. They often feel frightened, weary, and overwhelmed by the amount of effort involved in their treatment. Sometimes patients want to turn to something familiar and comfortable. Many return to their disease for relief. Relapses are common. But, they can be overcome. Nearly 90 percent of all patients treated for an eating disorder will significantly improve or recover. Two-thirds will do so within one to two years of treatment.

COPING WITH AN EATING DISORDER

When a friend or family member has an eating disorder, they need support. Sometimes that support is hard to give. A person with an eating disorder is likely to push family and friends away when they offer their help. It is important to remember how much people with this disease struggle. Frequently they experience urges to sneak away and purge, overexercise, or binge. Concerned friends and family members must try their best to be loyal, watchful, and caring. They should learn all they can about the disease and be ready to talk. They should keep conversations away from food and physical appearances. Families should store only healthy foods in the kitchen and gather regularly for meals. Friends and family should make themselves available for a walk, telephone call, or other distracting activities.

People with eating disorders can cope with their disease in many ways. By keeping a journal, they can recognize the events in their life that trigger their starving, bingeing, purging, or overexercising. If they can avoid these triggers, people will have harmful episodes less often. People struggling with the disease should focus on nutritious meals and not keep unhealthy food in the house. They should not shop alone. That makes them less likely to buy laxatives, diuretics, or high-calorie comfort foods.

If a person feels an urge to binge, purge, or overexercise, he or she should call a friend, walk the dog, take a bubble bath, see a movie, or watch a favorite television show. People with an eating disorder should avoid people who make them feel uncomfortable. They should build their self-esteem by giving themselves credit every time they resist even the smallest urge to binge, purge, or overexercise. Likewise, people with anorexia should feel good about themselves for eating a

Counselors who work with people with eating disorders help them learn to accept their normal body shape and size.

healthy meal. People with bulimia or binge-eating disorder should take pride when they resist a craving to eat when they are not actually hungry. They should also take heart when they eat to feed hunger, and stop when they feel full.

Secrecy and loneliness are a large part of an eating disorder. People with eating disorders should make every effort to socialize with friends and family. Most of all, people with eating disorders should recognize that their disease is serious and requires the help of friends, family, and health-care professionals. One professional advises that people move forward from a "blame-shame place" to an understanding that "we all hate the illness and we all love each other."

Doctors feel the greatest resource is communication between patients and their friends and family. Dena, a talented dancer suffered what she calls her "downward spiral" of anorexia for two years. Though her parents were worried, she told them all was well. But when her ballet teacher expressed concern, Dena confided in her. Yet, she continued starving until her teacher said that she was too unhealthy to dance in the state competition. Dena was off the team. With only her illness left,

For people with eating disorders treatment is often a long and difficult road. But with support and the proper medical and psychological advice, many find that they can stop their unhealthy eating habits and lead long and healthy lives.

Dena finally accepted the help of her parents. At 85 pounds and with a weakened heart, she was admitted to the hospital. Dena spent seven weeks learning how to eat, to communicate, to exercise in moderation, to love those that care for her, and to feel proud of her abilities. Her doctor is pleased at the progress Dena has made. She believes that her finest reward is being able to help people like Dena turn away from their disease and return to doing the great things they were meant to do.

Reaching Out

....

If you suspect a friend or classmate may have an eating disorder, the right thing to do is to get involved. Talk to your friend. Be careful not to sound critical, though. Start your sentences with "I" instead of "You". Here are some ways to express your concerns:

"I am worried about you because you haven't been eating lunch."
 or
"I heard that you were taking diet pills, and that makes me nervous."

Let your friend talk, if he or she will. Many people with eating disorders are quick to deny their disease. But, if you are honest and caring, it may be just the right time for your friend to confide in somebody.

Your friend may also ask that you keep it all a secret. Please encourage your friend to talk to a trusted adult—a teacher, nurse, counselor, parent, coach, or member of the clergy. Plan to go with your friend to lend your support. Remind your friend that eating disorders are extremely dangerous. You care a great deal about your friend and want to see your friend get well. Avoid talking about food or focusing on his or her appearance. Do not say, "You look sick" when your friend is dieting and do not say, "You look good" when he or she has gained a few pounds. The point is that you do not place value in your friend's appearances, but in his or her character.

If your conversation fails, your next step should be to tell a responsible adult about your friend's behavior. You are not being disloyal. Your friend's health, or maybe life, is at stake. Try expressing yourself this way:

"I'm worried about _____ because I saw her (or him) throw up on purpose."
"I'm afraid for _____, she (or he) never eats lunch."
"I'm concerned about _____. She (or He) is always down on herself (or himself) and is always talking about how fat she (or he) is."

Your friend needs professional care, and you can help.

GLOSSARY

amenorrhea—The loss of the menstrual periods; with eating disorders, usually caused by extreme weight loss and excessive exercise.

anorexia athletica—An eating disorder characterized by excessive exercise in order to lose weight.

anorexia nervosa—An eating disorder characterized by excessive dieting, self-starvation, and weight loss.

anti-depressants—Medication prescribed by doctors to ease the symptoms of depression and anxiety.

binge—To eat a large amount of food without control in a short amount of time.

body image—A mental picture of one's body.

bowels—Part of the digestive system.

bulimia nervosa—An eating disorder characterized by bingeing followed by purging in order to lose weight.

calorie—A shortened term for kilocalorie, an energy measurement used for food.

compulsive—Being unable to resist doing something, regardless of the outcome.

compulsive overeating—An eating disorder marked by frequent bouts of binge-eating and a feeling of loss of control.

depression—A psychological condition where a person feels unhappy and dissatisfied with life.

diuretic—A chemical that stimulates the body to rid itself of fluids by urination, also known as a water pill.

dehydration—When the body is depleted of fluids.

eating disorder—An unhealthy, out-of-control attitude towards weight, body size, food, and eating habits.

emetic—A solution that induces vomiting.

fast—To eat little or no food.

genes—Chemical information in the body that determine inherited traits.

genetics—The study of how characteristics are passed from parent to child.

hormones—Chemicals produced by the body that regulate growth and development.

lanugo—Fine, downy hairs that cover the body after excessive weight loss.

laxative—A chemical that stimulates the body to rid itself of wastes by defecation.

metabolism—Process of the body that breaks down food and turns it into energy.

nutrition—The process, or the study, of eating food and using it for growth and maintenance.

obese—Term used to describe a person who is very overweight and has a very large amount of extra body fat. Doctors use special calculations to determine obesity.

obsession—A psychological state when a person considers a particular thought or idea too often.

psychiatrist—A person with a medical doctor's degree in psychiatry, who helps people with mental, emotional, and behavioral disorders.

psychological—Having to do with the way people behave and think. Psychology is the study of mind and human behavior.

psychologist—A person with a graduate degree in psychology who helps people with problems of the mind and with the ways that people feel and act.

psychotherapy—Treating emotional and mental problems by talking, persuading, suggesting, and reassuring a patient.

puberty—The period when a person changes from child to adult and experiences rapid growth and development set off by hormones.

purge—In eating disorders, the act of getting rid of unwanted calories by vomiting, taking laxatives, using diuretics, or overexercising.

self-esteem—The thoughts and feelings a person has about himself or herself.

therapist—A health-care provider who helps patients with physical and emotional problems.

FIND OUT MORE

Organizations

Academy for Eating Disorders

60 Revere Drive, Suite 500

Northbrook, IL 60062-1577

(847) 498-4274

FAX: (847) 480-9282

http://www.aedweb.org

This international organization promotes excellence in research, treatment, and prevention of eating disorders.

Alliance for Eating Disorders Awareness

PO Box 13155

North Palm Beach, FL 33408-3155

(561) 841-0900

http://www.eatingdisorderinfo.org

The Alliance for Eating Disorders Awareness provides information and educational programs nationwide about the warning signs, dangers, and consequences of anorexia, bulimia, and other related eating disorders.

Dads and Daughters

34 East Superior St Suite 200

Duluth MN 55802

(888) 824-DADS

http://www.dadsanddaughters.org

Dads and Daughters is a national organization that improves and strengthens father-daughter relationships. Newsletters, books, and a Web site encourage fathers and daughters to discuss important issues such as media images and other cultural messages.

Eating Disorders Coalition

611 Pennsylvania Avenue SE #423

Washington, DC 20003-4303

(202) 543-9570

http://www.eatingdisorderscoalition.org

This organization urges lawmakers to recognize eating disorders as a public health issue.

National Association of Anorexia Nervosa and Associated Disorders (ANAD)

Box 7
Highland Park, IL 60035
Hotline: (847) 831-3438
http://www.anad.org/site/anadweb

ANAD offers counseling, a national network of free support groups, referrals to health care professionals, and education and prevention programs for eating disorders. ANAD works with health insurance companies to provide coverage for patients with eating disorders, encourages research, and fights negative advertising.

National Eating Disorders Association (NEDA)

603 Stewart Street, Suite 803
Seattle, WA 98101-1264
Toll-Free Hotline: (800) 931-2237
Phone: (206) 382-3587
http://www.nationaleatingdisorders.org

The National Eating Disorders Association is the largest nonprofit organization in the nation, dedicated to expanding public understanding of eating disorders and promoting access to quality treatment.

Books

Bode, Janet. *Food Fight : A Guide To Eating Disorders For Preteens And Their Parents*. New York: Simon & Schuster Books for Young Readers, 1997.

Harmon, Daniel E. *Anorexia Nervosa: Starving For Attention*. Philadelphia, PA: Chelsea House Publishers, 1999.

Kaminker, Laura. *Exercise Addiction: When Fitness Becomes An Obsession*. New York: Rosen Publishing, 1998.

Kubersky, Rachel. *Everything You Need To Know About Eating Disorders: Anorexia And Bulimia*. New York: Rosen Publishing, 1996.

Moe, Barbara. *Inside Eating Disorder Support Groups*. New York: Rosen Publishing, 1998.

Normandi, Carol Emery. *Over It:A Teen's Guide To Getting Beyond Obsession With Food And Weight*. Novato, CA: New World Library, 2001.

Turck, Mary. *Food And Emotions*. Mankato, MN: LifeMatters, 2001.

Web Sites

Anorexia Nervosa and Related Eating Disorders, Inc. (ANRED)
http://www.anred.com

The Center for Eating Disorders
http://www.eating-disorders.com

Eating Disorder Referral and Information Center
http://www.edreferral.com

KidsHealth
http://kidshealth.org/kid/health_problems/learning_
  problem/eatdisorder.html

The Renfrew Center Foundation
http://www.renfrewcenter.com/for-you/index.asp

INDEX

Page numbers for illustrations are in **boldface**

ABOUT THE AUTHOR

Ruth Bjorklund lives on Bainbridge Island in Puget Sound with her husband and two children. She has written several books for young people. In researching this book, she has met numerous caring individuals: teachers, coaches, nurses, doctors, and other community members who are dedicated to the health and well-being of children.